THE ALGONQUIN

BAR AND COCKTAIL BOOK

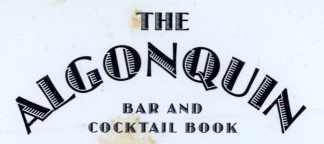

ANNA KIERNAN

BARNES & NOBLE BOOKS
NEW YORK

With love and thanks to the Kiernans,
especially Sadie, Francis, Pam, Nora, and Austen.

A QUINTET BOOK

**This edition published by
Barnes & Noble, Inc.
By arrangement with Quintet Books Ltd
2002 Barnes & Noble Books**

Library of Congress Cataloging Data available upon request.

ISBN 0 7607 3497 6

M 10 9 8 7 6 5 4 3 2 1

**This book was designed and produced by
Quintet Publishing Limited
6 Blundell Steet
London N7 9BH**

Photography Jeremy Thomas
Designer Jon Wainwright
Editor Erin Connell
Managing Editor Diana Steedman
Creative Director Richard Dewing
Publisher Oliver Salzmann

Manufactured in Singapore by Universal Graphics Pte Ltd
Printed in China by Winner Printing and Packaging Ltd

NOTE
*Because of the slight risk of salmonella, raw eggs should not be
served to the very young, the ill or elderly, or to pregnant women.

CONTENTS

INTRODUCTION

Every cocktail has a story, and almost every storyteller, it would seem, has a cocktail. Which may be why the history of cocktails is so colorful.

Tinctures, mixtures, and concoctions akin to the cocktail have been prepared since people have been able to drink and think. A Roman doctor, Claudius, made reference to a blend of wine, lemon juice, and dried herbs, which he called "cockwine," and the emperor (Lucius Aelius Aurelius) concurred that this was an excellent drink. Plato believed that intoxication revealed the truth of a man's inner self, and Homer never wrote without partaking of a drop of something first.

The true rise of the cocktail, though, runs parallel with the advent of the Enlightenment and Industrial Revolution, from the late eighteenth century onwards. As Oscar Wilde said, "Work is the curse of the drinking class." And, as workforces surged towards the cities, Gin Palaces, public houses, and illicit drinking dens flourished.

The first known written references to cocktails can be found in the New York newspaper *The Balance and Columbian Repository*, in 1806:

"Cocktail is a stimulating liquor, composed of spirits of any kind, sugar, water, and bitters – it is vulgarly called bittered sling and is supposed to be an excellent electioneering potion."

The origins of the cocktail are a moot point, though there is much evidence to suggest that the cocktail is an American invention. The title of John Bartlett's 1848 *Dictionary of Americanisms*, which includes a definition of the cocktail, suggests as much, and the most persuasive stories hold with this assertion. John MacQueen sees the Revolutionary War as the birthplace of the drink. At the time, the innkeeper of the Bunch of Grapes, Squire Allen, lost his prized fighting cock, Jupiter. When the bird was returned, Allen celebrated with a toast to the "cock's tail" since the bird's feathers were barely ruffled by his adventure! Or perhaps the cocktail can be traced back to Monsieur Antoine

Peychaud, a New Orleans chemist, who served guests drinks in eggcups, and those drinks possibly contained tonics from his pharmacy. The French word for eggcup is *coquetier*, and Peychaud bitters are an alternative to Angostura bitters. This may offer a more watertight cocktail tale.

Prohibition (1920-1933) fired America's thirst for cocktails. Dissenters caught up in the slipstream of illegal drinking dens consumed dastardly blends with abandon. Of course, the cocktail was the bootlegger's partner in crime, since moonshine and its less well-bred relations needed to be disguised to be drunk.

The Prohibition ended with a gala party in January 1933 in the lobby of the Algonquin Hotel. It was led by two of the leading musical comedy stars of the era – Marilyn Miller and Clifton Webb (who later filmed a scene from the great film *Laura* in the hotel's Round Table Room, opposite Gene Tierney).

Even then, the Algonquin Hotel's most noteworthy cocktail was the Martini, served in the world-renowned Blue Bar. Years later, H. L. Mencken declared the Martini, to be, "the only American invention as perfect as a sonnet."

According to leading London mixologist Angus Winchester, "The British don't really have a cocktail-bar culture, which means we're often more creative because we are not limited by tradition." Despite this, cocktails have evolved as an upper class aperitif for British writers such as Evelyn Waugh (see page 40) – a tipple to be taken after high tea and before supper.

While Gin and Tonics and Pimms seemed to serve best the pleasures of the English Gentleman abroad, cocktails have always captured the imagination of youth. While speakeasies were swinging in the United States, so the Bright Young Things in Britain were enjoying their own concoctions.

That cocktails are still a style statement is no great surprise. Attitudes have changed, though: mixology is now viewed as something of an art, and good bartenders have cult followings in trendy bars. The cocktail's renaissance is reminiscent of the heady 1920s and 1930s, but with a new breed of bartenders reinventing classic recipes.

Elle magazine tells its readers to drink a Raspberry Martini "With panache. Hold the stem with your index finger supporting the slope of the glass to avoid spillage down your décolletage." Whereas apparently drinking a Mojito tells the world that "If it's in vogue, it's in your hand."

The bartender's sentiments in *Cocktail: A Strong Drink in Three Acts*, published in 1935, speak of a rather different modern woman:

"Everything's fast, nowadays ... take the Modern Woman, for instance: she has on her men the same effect of the Modern Drink: first she stuns them, then she excites them, and, after a time, she evaporates, leaving them alone in the morning, with an empty mind and a strong headache."

Despite changes in the social makeup of the drinker, as with all matters of style, the cocktail is a timeless creation. And as with all great pleasures, it will continue to be reinvented and revisited.

Nobody is altogether sure of the source of the cocktail. But the purpose is clear: an agreeably sophisticated means of getting rather drunk. As Lord Byron put it so succinctly: **"Man, being reasonable, must get drunk; the best of life is but intoxication."**

THE ALGONQUIN HOTEL

"Drunkenness in good literature is not like drunkenness in real life; it is subtly spiritualised ..."
J. B. PRIESTLEY

The Algonquin Hotel in New York City played host to some of the most riveting raconteurs of modern times. The home of the legendary Round Table (or vicious circle, as it was less favorably known) in the Roaring Twenties, the Algonquin welcomed writers, artists, and eminent intellectuals to its renowned Rose Room. There they would banter, gossip, and debate, so that the air was full of sweet-and-sour acerbic exchanges. With a captivating cast including drama critic Robert Benchley, actors Harpo Marx and Tallulah Bankhead, and writer

"A Round Table Indeed!" by Natalie Ascencios. Among the noted celebrities around the Table are Harpo Marx, George S. Kaufman, Dorothy Parker, Robert Benchley, Edna Ferber and Franklin Pierce Adams.

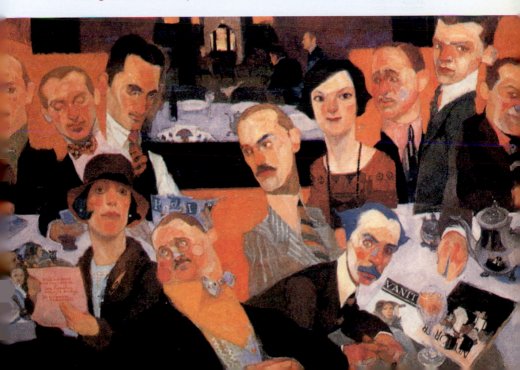

Dorothy Parker, the Algonquin was witness to an unprecedented era of sparkling conversations, satirical asides, and absurdist interludes.

While many of us might entertain the notion that we are more captivating while under the influence, the effervescence of this particular group is undisputed and remains a source of inspiration for would-be creative spirits. To be reserved when spurred on by a couple of fine Martinis is an art; to be understated in the presence of genius, a rare talent, as Robert Benchley suggests: "It took me 15 years to discover that I had no talent for writing, but I couldn't give it up because by that time I was too famous."

The Algonquin group thrived in an era when economic depression, the prohibition of alcohol, and wars were creating a taut society fraught with the tensions of everyday life. With the adoption of the Eighteenth Amendment to the Constitution, the prohibition of alcohol became the law of the land, and the United States

The Blue Bar of the Algonquin Hotel. The hotel's lounge rooms are evocative of the Roaring Twenties. and today it is the place to see and be seen. in a setting that relives some of America´s glory days.

was split between those in favor of a "dry" country and those who supported a "wet" society.

For many, the aspirational blend of indolent pleasure and unforgiving satire displayed by the Algonquin-ites caught the imagination in a climate of enforced austerity. Perhaps what made this particular literary coterie so likeable was their lack of pomposity combined with a love – and lust – for life. Alexander Woollcott's "I must get out of these wet words and into the Dry Martini" is a phrase in point.

The legend of the Algonquin holds a similar appeal today. The subversive stream of ideas running through the Rose Room in the 1920s and 1930s stands in sharp contrast to the functionality of today's media, and perhaps of the workplace in general, where pace and production are paramount. A few literary establishments remain that honor the traditions bestowed upon their profession. The staff at Britain's satirical magazine *Private Eye*, for instance, still make their weekly way to The Coach and Horses in Soho, London, where their editorial meetings take place. But this is something of an exception to the new rules of play.

This book draws together two of the most potent pleasures of modern life: good literature and good cocktails. The marriage of the two is inevitable, because, conversely, it is the nature of genius to be in possession of an enquiring mind that craves to be altered. Such transformations are usually achieved through escapism rendered possible by illicit substances, religion, or love. Verlaine and Rimbaud's pursuit of pleasure was almost religious in its fervor, which can be seen in the latter's words, "The Road of Excess leads to the Palace of Wisdom". Here Rimbaud notes, "Knowing pilgrims, seek repose/By the emerald pillars of Absinthe…"

But cocktails offer more than mere escapism; they are decadent distractions, mischievous asides, and elegant rewards. Ultimately, the cocktail is a sociable drink, and to be enjoyed in pleasant circumstances and in the finest company. As the literary anecdotes in this volume decry, a cocktail is a thing to be savored and remembered, a point well noted by Kingsley Amis:

"I drank my first Dry Martini in a New York cocktail bar…America has given the world nothing finer or more cheering than this classic drink, not even jazz."

ESSENTIALS

Like almost everything in life, cocktail essentials are to some extent a matter of personal preference. While Vernon Heaton insists in *Cocktail Party Secrets* that, "Each guest should have a minimum of 4ft by 4ft in which to stand," do not fret if your home is less than palatial.

Preparation is everything when planning a cocktail party, but there is no need to become obsessive, or you'll be unlikely to enjoy yourself. And fun, lest we forget, should be the defining factor of any cocktail party.

ICE

"Ice
Never use twice
Wake your shaker!
Ice your glasses."
SAVVY ADVICE INDEED FROM
THE SAVOY MIXOLOGISTS.

I cannot emphasize enough how important it is to have a plentiful supply of ice when preparing cocktails. Anyone who says they don't mind drinking their cocktail warm doesn't deserve one.

MEASURES

The liquid content of the recipes in this book are divided into "parts." Where one part represents one jigger, two parts represents two jiggers, and so forth. I find this to be the most user-friendly type of recipe, since it makes multiplying quantities easy. It also saves you from dillydallying with measurements and allows you to prepare good cocktails quickly. Nobody wants to wait long for their drink, and drawn out preparations at a party can distract from what matters most: ensuring that everyone is having a good time. As master mixologist Harry Craddock said, the best way to drink a cocktail is "quickly, while it's laughing at you!"

Jigger – 2 fl oz (50 ml)
Dash – 6 drops
Teaspoon – 1 teaspoon (5 ml)
Pint – 2 1/2 cups (570 ml)
Fifth – 4 cups (950 ml)
Quart – 5 cups (1.3 l)
Juice of 1 lemon – 1 fl oz (30 ml)

GLASSES

Cocktail glasses should reflect the style of the drink. A Martini served in an Old-Fashioned glass is quite simply wrong. And a cocktail served in a warm or smeared glass is a waste of a cocktail.

Cocktails are cool, so your glass should be too! If you don't have space in your refrigerator, either fill your cocktail glass with shaved ice before using (this will frost the glass and give it that sublime, smoky appearance), or place it in the freezer or your ice bucket for a few moments beforehand.

Sugar frosting is when the rim is wetted, usually with citrus fruit, then dipped into sugar. The same method can be used with salt when making Margaritas.

Sling
8–10 fl oz
(1 cup/235 ml)

Champagne flute
4 fl oz (1/2 cup/120 ml)

Highball/Collins
8–10 fl oz
(1 cup/235 ml)

Rocks
12 fl oz (1 cup/235 ml)

Old-Fashioned
4–8 fl oz
(^{1}/$_2$–1 cup/120–235 ml)

Shot
1–2 fl oz
(^{1}/$_4$ cup/50 ml)

Wine
4 fl oz (^{1}/$_2$ cup/120 ml)

Margarita
4 fl oz (^{1}/$_2$ cup/120 ml)

Martini/Cocktail
4 fl oz (^{1}/$_2$ cup/120 ml)

BAR FIXTURES

VITAL

Shaker

You shouldn't even consider making cocktails without the obligatory cocktail shaker. Shaken cocktails tend to be frothier affairs with more volume. Using crushed ice will increase your quantity too, and will ensure that your drinks are ice cold.

Jigger (spirit measure)

The jigger (or one part) is equivalent to a shot which measures 2 fluid ounces (or $1/4$ cup/50 ml).

Bottle opener and corkscrew

Ice bucket

A cocktail needs ice like a fish needs water. Ice buckets can also be used to chill glasses before use.

DESIRABLE

Cutting board and paring knife

Fruit

Always use fresh fruit and juice. The only exception to this rule is keeping slices of lemon and orange in the freezer. This will save you time when preparing cocktails, and also further chills the drink.

Lemons and limes should be kept in plentiful supply, since the zest and peel are essential for some drinks. For fruity cocktails, always add the alcohol last, so it slides through the citrus juice rather than sitting at the base of the drink.

Juicer

Juice extractors are incredibly useful for preparing deliciously different drinks with fresh fruit. Be warned though – there is no getting around the fact that they are a nightmare to clean.

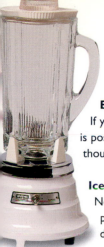

Blender

If you don't have a blender, it is possible to push soft fruit though a strainer.

Ice tongs

Nobody wants your mucky paws sullying their silky drink! Ice tongs help.

Bar spoon

As we all know, certain drinks are shaken, not stirred. Clear cocktails should be stirred, but a brisk, steady stir is all that is required. Stir too much and you lose the fizz and melt the ice, stir too little and you have an unmixed drink.

Waiter's friend

This is a very useful gadget since it combines a corkscrew, bottle opener, and knife.

Cocktail sticks

For skewering cherries, olives, and other garnishes.

Cocktail stirrers

Decorative and functional, kitschy cocktail stirrers are a cute addition to any cocktail cabinet.

GOMME (SUGAR SYRUP)

Preparing this yourself is easy, though it can be purchased.

1 Place 1 cup of sugar and 1 cup of water in a pan and bring to a boil.
2 Reduce heat and simmer gently until the mixture condenses into a clear, sweet syrup. This will take approximately 5 minutes.
3 Cool. Store in a sealed container in the refrigerator.

GIN-BASED COCKTAILS

Gin is a drink with a fascinating past. One of the first literary references to it can be found in Shakespeare's *Henry VII*, but since Elizabethan times, gin's social and cultural significance has metamorphosed more than once.

Gin first gained popular status when the Dutch William of Orange ruled England with his wife Mary II. They raised taxes on alcoholic imports from France as a rebuke for French hostilities in Holland, and gin became the cheap alternative.

Gin Palaces subsequently grew increasingly popular among the working classes in Britain during the second half of the nineteenth century. Despite Prime Minister Gladstone's abject dislike for Gin Palaces, the public outcry against his actions (he sought to halve their number in 1871) meant he had to withdraw his puritanical proposals or risk alienating the electorate.

Elsewhere, gin was fast becoming the preferred drink of those exploring Africa and India. It had been discovered as an admirable base with which to mix quinine water, an anti-malarial elixir. The blend is of course gin and tonic, one of the few cocktails to combine medicinal properties with a sublime drink.

Juniper berries, most commonly grown in Tuscany, Italy, are the most common source of gin's distinctive taste. (In the 18th century, juniper berries were wrongly believed to induce miscarriages, hence the term for gin "Mother's ruin.")

London Dry gin can be produced anywhere, but to earn the name, the base spirit must be rectified to neutrality before being redistilled with the botanical flavorings for which the drink is renowned. Even so, a request for a "gin and tonic" today seems as quintessentially English as "anyone for tennis?"

IMPERIAL

The Imperial cocktail is the potent concoction with a cameo role in *Remember?* The classic 1939 film sees a love triangle beset by amnesia, in which Greer Garson (Linda) takes her first starring role. Jeff and Linda fall in love twice because of the amnesia-inducing drink, which renders their first fall false.
A little like *A Midsummer Night's Dream, Remember?* warns against the dangers of mixing intoxication and intimacy, particularly when dealing with "Mother's ruin."
You have been warned!

1 part gin
1 part dry vermouth
Dash of Angostura bitters
Dash of maraschino cherry juice
1 green olive

Shake the ingredients and pour into an iced martini glass. Finish with an olive.

GIMLET

The Gimlet replenished tired adventurers in Hemingway's *The Snows of Kilimanjaro* (1952). But while Papa Hemingway was said to be fond of the cocktail, he was rumored to be less sure of the screen adaptation of his novel…

2 parts gin
1 part lime cordial

Shake and pour into an iced martini glass.

Tip
You can replace the gin with vodka.

MAIDEN'S BLUSH

2 parts gin
4 dashes of curaçao
4 dashes of grenadine
Dash of lemon juice
Ice
Slice of lemon

Shake with ice and strain into a cocktail glass. Garnish with lemon slice.

Tip
Add a teaspoon each of sugar and raspberry syrup if you desire a sweeter, deeper blush.

BROADWAY SPECIAL

"Of all the gin joints in all the towns in the world she had to walk into mine."
RICK BLAIN, *CASABLANCA (1942)*

Hollywood's longstanding affair with the cocktail is undisputed. The two combine a seductive blend of escapism and entertainment, which began during Prohibition in the 1920s, and continues today with the delightful decadence of Carrie Bradshaw and the women of *Sex and the City*.

The Broadway Special brings together all the ingredients that make this special relationship work. And for actors who want to stay slender, they'll find that with nutmeg, egg white, and pineapple juice, this is virtually a meal in itself!
"Here's looking at you, kid!"

2 parts gin
1 part sweet vermouth
1 teaspoon pineapple juice
2 dashes of grenadine
1/2 egg white
Pinch of grated nutmeg
Ice
Fresh pineapple

Shake ingredients with ice and strain into a chilled cocktail glass. Add some fresh pineapple for a big production number.

SUNSHINE COCKTAIL

1 dash **Angostura bitters**
1 part **vermouth**
2 parts **dry gin**
Orange juice
Orange peel

Stir and strain. Add a twist of orange peel to glass.

SINGAPORE SLING

Ngiam Tong Boon, bartender at Raffles Hotel's infamous long bar, is said to have invented this drink. Now an undisputed classic, this beguiling blend was said to be a favorite with suitably distinguished writers Somerset Maugham and Joseph Conrad.

1 part **gin**
1 part **cherry brandy**
$^1/_2$ part **Cointreau**
$^1/_2$ part **Bénédictine**
$^1/_2$ part **lime juice**
7 parts **orange juice**
7 parts **pineapple juice**
Ice
Slice of pineapple

Shake and strain into a highball or Collins glass. This exotic cocktail should be finished with a slice of pineapple and lots of ice.

If necessary, it's possible to do without the Cointreau and Bénédictine by topping off with soda instead, but you will lose the drink's delightfully different flavor by doing so.

GIN RICKEY

"Tom came back, preceding four Gin Rickeys that clicked full of ice. Gatsby took up his drink.
'They certainly look cool,'
he said, with visible tension.
We drank in long, greedy swallows."
FROM *THE GREAT GATSBY*
BY F. SCOTT FITZGERALD

The Gin Rickey is a disarmingly unassuming little number – perfect for long afternoons spent in the summer sun.

2 parts gin
4 parts soda water
Juice of 1 lime
Ice
Lime wedge

Squeeze the lime juice over plenty of ice in a tall glass. Add the gin and stir before adding the soda water, stir again, then add a lime wedge to garnish.

NEGRONI

"I never drink anything stronger than gin before breakfast."
W. C. FIELDS

1 part Campari
1 part gin
1 part sweet vermouth
Ice
Twist of lemon peel

Stir with ice in a mixing glass, then strain into a cocktail glass and add a lemon twist.

TOM COLLINS

There are a number of versions of this old-fashioned classic. An authentic TC should be made with Old Tom gin, but since this brand is only available in the Far East, London Dry Gin can be used instead. Sticklers will tell you that this is, in fact, a John Collins, but see if they can tell the difference!

2 parts gin
1 part lemon juice
Sugar cube
Chilled soda water
Ice
Slice of orange or lemon

Stir the gin, sugar, and lemon juice with ice in a Collins glass. Top off with soda water. Stir and add the citrus slice of your choice.

WHISKY-BASED COCKTAILS

"'Let's have another drink,'
Nick said.
'It's Scotch,' he said.
Bill had poured out the
drinks...
'What'll we drink to?' Nick
asked, holding up the
glass.
'Let's drink to fishing,'
Bill said...
They drank all that was in
their glasses...
Nick poured out the liquor.
Bill poured in the water.
They looked at each other.
They felt very fine."

FROM *THE THREE DAY BLOW* BY
ERNEST HEMINGWAY

Whisky or whiskey, however you spell it, is the drink of serious drinkers. Lady of letters Simone de Beauvoir claimed that, "I have two or three Scotches during the day," and viewed whisky as a "necessary" passion, a belief she shared with her muse, Jean Paul Sartre.

Even the debate between Scottish *whisky* and Irish *whiskey* continues among evangelical supporters of both camps. Its translation from the Gaelic – "water of life" – has a certain gravitas that a Piña Colada could never compete with. What joy, then, to lighten up this heavy nectar with the wayward cocktails in this section!

Legend has it that the Irish were the first to make whisky, and that their distilling techniques were taken by monks to Scotland in the early Middle Ages.

Rye whiskey made its debut in the United States when Irish and Scottish immigrants came to the New World in the seventeenth century. To earn its name, it must be made up of a minimum of 51 percent rye. Bourbon is the American equivalent produced in the South, and tends to be heavier than Canadian varieties.

Scotch is blended, and the distinctive smoky flavor comes from drying the malted barley over peat fires. The malt in Irish whiskey is dried in coal-fired kilns and the aroma tends to be heavier than that produced by the Scottish method.

Single malts should be drunk neat, be they bourbon, whisky, or whiskey. So bear in mind that there's no point in wasting a good single malt on a cocktail, lest an expert be waiting in the wings for a chance to soliloquize on the subject!

THE ALGONQUIN

*"I like to have a martini
Two at the very most.
After three I'm under the
table.
After four I'm under the
host."*
DOROTHY PARKER

**3 parts whisky
I part dry vermouth
I part pineapple juice
Ice**

Add the ingredients to a shaker half-filled with ice. Shake and strain over ice into a cocktail glass.

This unassuming cocktail should be the little star of any self-respecting mixologist's cocktail repertoire. Combining an unlikely blend of whisky and pineapple, The Algonquin is hard-hitting and refreshing in equal measure. Just imagine the intellectual knights of the Algonquin Round Table settling down for some serious debate, spurred on by this favorite. With wits such as Dorothy Parker present, it seems unlikely that much tedious talk passed over that particular table.

COWBOY COCKTAIL

2 parts rye whisky
1 part heavy cream
Cracked ice

Shake the whisky and cream with
cracked ice, then strain into a
cocktail glass.

RUSTY NAIL

2 parts Scotch whisky
1 part Drambuie
Ice

Pour the Scotch, then the Drambuie,
over ice into an old-fashioned glass.

WHISKY MAC

"Giv me a visky, ginger ale on the side, and don't be stingy, baby."
GRETA GARBO'S FIRST SPEAKING ROLE IN THE FILM *ANNA CHRISTIE* (1930)

1 part **Scotch whisky**
2 parts **ginger wine (or ginger ale)**
Ice
Twist of lemon peel

Pour the whisky and wine (or ale) over ice in an old-fashioned glass. To finish, twist the lemon peel over it.

WHISKY SOUR

"I'm perfectly capable of fixing my own breakfast. As a matter of fact, I had two peanut butter sandwiches and two Whisky Sours."
RICHARD SHERMAN (TOM EWELL) IN *THE SEVEN YEAR ITCH* (1955)

2 parts **bourbon (or rye whisky)**
Juice of two lemons
1 **egg white**
Sugar syrup
2 dashes of **Angostura bitters**
Ice

Add the lemon juice to the egg white, then mix with whisky, a small measure of sugar syrup, and the bitters. Shake with ice in shaker and serve in an old-fashioned glass.

Tip
For a fancy finish, garnish with a stemmed cherry.

SCOTCH MIST

Bogart and Bacall drink this in *The Big Sleep* (1946), William Faulkner's adaptation of Raymond Chandler's novel. This is the haiku of the cocktail kingdom.

2 parts Scotch whisky
Ice
Twist of lemon peel

Shake the Scotch with ice, then strain into a champagne glass. Finally, twist the peel over it.

WARD EIGHT

Despite the perplexing connotations of its name, a splash of this sprightly drink will perk you up in no time!

2 parts bourbon
I part lemon juice
I part orange juice
Dash of grenadine
Cracked ice

Shake with cracked ice and strain into a chilled cocktail glass.

HOT TODDY

"I'm not living with you. We occupy the same cage, that's all."

In *Cat on a Hot Tin Roof*, legendary leads Liz Taylor and Paul Newman play angst-ridden Brick and Maggie Pollit. This powerful adaptation of Tennessee Williams's exposé of marital strife, cancer, and repressed sexuality is temporarily tempered by Hot Toddies! Imagine, then, what it can do for a common cold!

Double Scotch whisky (2 parts)
1 tablespoon honey
Juice of 1 lemon
Rind of 1 lemon
Cinnamon stick
1 cup of boiling water
5 whole cloves
Slice of lemon
Pinch of ground cinnamon

Put the whisky and honey in a heatproof rocks glass with the lemon juice, rind and cinnamon stick. Add the boiling water and stir. Stick the cloves into skin of lemon slice and put in glass. Sprinkle with cinnamon to garnish.

MANHATTAN

There are numerous versions of this elegant little cocktail, so play around with it to find your perfect Manhattan. A Rob Roy is the Scottish equivalent, but somehow it just doesn't have quite the same ring…

2 parts whisky
1 part sweet vermouth
Dash of angostura bitters
Ice

Stir with ice in a mixing glass then strain into a chilled cocktail glass.

Tip
A Francophile variation uses dry vermouth and a dash of Cointreau. Add a maraschino cherry if you desire.

BARBARY COAST

And to finish? This unapologetically decadent late night treat!

2 parts Scotch whisky
1 part gin
1 part crème de cacao
Ice
1 part heavy cream
Grated nutmeg, chocolate,
or both!

Pour the whisky, gin and crème de cacao over the ice in your shaker. Add the cream and shake hard. Pour into an old-fashioned glass and garnish.

RUM-BASED COCKTAILS

"We put all the bottles on
an empty bookshelf and
sometimes there were as
many as twenty or thirty...it
was a good feeling to have a
stock of rum that would
never run out..."
HUNTER S. THOMPSON,
THE RUM DIARIES

Rum is a sunshine drink which reminds me of balmy evenings overlooking the ocean while on Tortola, an island in the Caribbean. The root of many ostentatious cocktails, rum is not a shy spirit, or one for the fainthearted.

Rum is a compelling part of the history of colonial trading between Europe and the New World. Immortalized in the words of Robert Louis Stevenson in *Treasure Island*, "Yo-ho-ho and a bottle of rum!" the drink is derived from sugar cane and still comprises a staple export from the West Indies.

Thompson's heady novel, *The Rum Diaries*, is both a barfly's confessional and a cultural comment on how integral rum was to Puerto Rican life in the 1950s. Rum bars stretched along entire streets, where the drink was traditionally a working class staple drunk straight. In contrast, the new moneyed classes' consumption is critiqued: "To go to a cocktail party in San Juan was to see all that was cheap and greedy in human nature…"

Less well known, though, are rum's affiliations with Australia, where the spirit is the national drink, or in Newfoundland, where a rough version of the drink, known as Screech, was exchanged for cod in the nineteenth century, and is still drunk in the region today.

Despite the variety of rums available, the main split is between dark and light rum.

Light rums (including white rums) are generally harsher tasting and less expensive than dark rums. Dark rums are aged in oak casks, and, like whisky, those aged longer tend to have a fuller flavor.

While the Martini is the elegant aunt of the cocktail family, and whisky the venerable uncle, so rum is the wayward child – irrepressible and quite delicious!

DAIQUIRI

"He had drunk double frozen daiquiris, the great ones...that had no taste of alcohol and felt, as you drank them, the way downhill skiing feels running through powder snow and, after the sixth and eighth, felt like downhill glacier skiing feels when you are running unroped."
FROM *ISLANDS IN THE STREAM* BY ERNEST HEMINGWAY

Legend has it that Ernest Hemingway broke the record for the number of double daiquiris drunk at the Hotel Foridita in Havana, Cuba. It was also the drink of choice in the film *To Have and Have Not* (1944) where Humphrey Bogart's character, Steve Morgan, was rumored to have been based on Joe Russell, owner of Sloppy Joe's bar, also in Havana, Cuba. In fact, the predilection of Hemingway's infamous characters for the drink makes the distinction between fact and fiction as blurry as a double-daiquiri drinker's vision.

2 parts white rum
$2/3$ part lime juice
1 teaspoon superfine sugar
Ice
1 slice of lime

Fill half the shaker with ice cubes. Add the superfine sugar, lime juice, and rum. Shake and strain into a well-chilled cocktail glass. Garnish with a lime slice.

For a frozen, Hemingway-style version, simply put crushed ice in your glass and then strain the ingredients into it.

Tip
In current cocktail practice, it is now acceptable to replace rum with vodka.

MAI TAI

"Careful, Daddy: those Mai Tais can be mighty powerful."

CHAD GATES (ELVIS PRESLEY) IN *BLUE HAWAII* (1961)

Looks can be deceiving. While the Mai Tai seems all sweet and innocent – not unlike Elvis, who was a teetotaler himself – this is a deceptively potent drink. The flirtatious younger sister of the Daiquiri, this drink is a little more complicated but also commensurately rewarding.

2 parts gold rum
2 parts dark rum
I part curaçao
Dash of orgeat syrup (almond syrup)
Juice of I lime
Dash of Angostura bitters
Ice
Twist of lime peel
Pineapple pieces
Fresh mint

Pour ingredients over ice in an old-fashioned or Collins glass, or a hollowed-out pineapple. Stir, then garnish with lime peel, pineapple pieces, and mint.

PLANTER'S COCKTAIL

Planter's Cocktail is the country cousin of Planter's Punch, and was a popular thirst quencher in the American South at the turn of the twentieth century. It is immortalized in the 1939 film, *Gone With the Wind*, in which Scarlett O'Hara (Vivien Leigh) and Rhett Butler's (Clark Gable) heated emotions are quelled by this cooling drink.

1 part rum
1 part orange juice
Dash of lemon juice

Shake and strain over lots of ice in an old-fashioned glass.

Variation:

¹/₂ part lemon juice
¹/₂ part simple syrup
1 part rum

You can top up with Angostura bitters or soda water if you so desire.

MOJITO

Like a Mojito, the screen version of Graham Greene's novel, *Our Man in Havana*, possesses a twist. Jim Wormold (Sir Alec Guinness) is a Hoover salesman in Havana who becomes part of the British Secret Service by default.

This is a simple and sublime cocktail, a perfect drink at the end of a long, hard day!

2 parts gold rum
Dash of lime juice
Dash of sugar syrup
Soda water
5 fresh mint leaves
Shaved ice

Mix mint and rum thoroughly; add shaved ice, lime, and sugar syrup. Top up with soda water and stir.

PIÑA COLADA

Rum cocktails offer divine after-dinner decadence. The Piña Colada – when made properly and comprising of fresh ingredients – is a delicious alternative (or addition!) to dessert. The Peenie, as it is affectionately known, is a justifiably showy drink, so don't be afraid to dress it up with a cherry, chunk of pineapple, and a cocktail umbrella!

1 part light rum
1 part coconut cream
2 parts pineapple juice
Crushed ice

Pour the rum, coconut cream, and pineapple juice over the ice in the shaker and shake well. Strain into a chilled Collins glass and decorate as desired with Maraschino cherry, pineapple chunk, straw, and cocktail umbrella.

ZOMBIE

"Promise me one thing: don't take me home until I'm drunk – very drunk indeed."
HOLLY GOLIGHTLY (AUDREY HEPBURN) IN *BREAKFAST AT TIFFANY'S* (1961)

Truman Capote's portrait of the entirely enigmatic Holly Golightly is as astute in its portrayal of "phonies" as Salinger's *The Catcher in the Rye* ever was. Like Holly, the Zombie is testament to unfettered hedonism. Its effects are recalled in that magical moment where a statuesque guest at Holly's soirée topples, to Holly's delighted cry of "Timber!"

1 part light rum
1 part dark rum
1 part Jamaican rum
1 part over-proof rum
Fresh passion fruit juice
Fresh pineapple juice
Sugar syrup
Ice

Shake and strain into a highball glass of ice.

ACAPULCO

This is a subtle sweet-and-sour blend, for which fresh pineapple is essential.

1 part golden rum
$^{1}/_{2}$ part Cointreau
2 parts pineapple juice
Juice of 1 lime
Crushed ice
Pineapple

Shake with crushed ice and pour into cocktail glasses. Garnish with cubed pineapple.

BRANDY-BASED COCKTAILS

"For two intimates, lovers or comrades, to spend a quiet evening with nothing but a glass of cognac is the ideal."
EVELYN WAUGH'S ADVICE IN *VOGUE*, 1965.

Although viewed by his contemporaries as a brilliant satirist, Waugh is perhaps best known for his 1945 novel *Brideshead Revisited*, in which the decline of the aristocracy is traced through the exploits of the novel's two pleasure-seeking leads:

"'Ought we to be drunk every night,' Sebastian asked one morning.
'Yes, I think so.'
'I think so too.'"

Brandy is undoubtedly the most understated and seductive of the spirits family. Part of the appeal of this golden liquid is that it floods the drinker with a momentary warmth similar to the flutter of butterflies felt in the first flush of romance.

Bought cheap and drunk straight in wine-making regions of Spain, the more distinguished varieties, such as Armagnac and Cognac, are French, and should not be served with an ice cube or imbibed as part of a cocktail. Brandy can also be prepared from other fruits such as apples (Calvados) and cherries (kirschwasser) and can contain up to 55 percent alcohol.

MOULIN ROUGE

" 'Please, maman, don't move! I'm going to do your portrait.'
'What, another one! But, Henri, you just did my portrait yesterday.'
Adèle, Comtesse de Toulouse-Lautrec, rested her embroidery in the lap of her crinoline and smiled down at the little boy crouched before her on the lawn."

2 parts apricot brandy
1 part orange juice
1 part lemon juice
3 dashes of grenadine

Shake well and strain into cocktail glasses.

So begins Pierre La Mure's *Moulin Rouge: A Novel based on the life of Henri de Toulouse-Lautrec*. Suffice to say that the cocktail is less La Mure and more Luhrmann, since, like Baz Luhrmann's film *Moulin Rouge*, the drink is a carnival-esque celebration rather than a still life.

BRANDY ALEXANDER

In *The Life of Samuel Johnson*, James Boswell observes that, **"He who aspires to be a hero must drink brandy."**

2 parts brandy
1 part dark crème de cacao
1 part heavy cream
Ice
A grating of nutmeg, to garnish

Shake ingredients with ice, strain into a cocktail glass, and decorate with nutmeg.

VALENCIA COCKTAIL

2 parts apricot brandy
1 part orange juice
4 dashes of orange bitters

Shake with ice and strain into a cocktail glass.

CHARLESTON

"Life is a luminous halo, a semi-transparent envelope surrounding us from the beginning of consciousness to the end."

FROM *THE COMMON READER* BY VIRGINIA WOOLF

Legend has it that this drink was a favorite among the flappers who took to the dance floor in the 1920s. Personally, I prefer to associate the drink with the home of Virginia Woolf, Quentin Bell, Vanessa Bell, *et al*, a charming retreat in the heart of Sussex, England. But dancing and drinking are not so very different when done well, and it's to be supposed that with the aid of this little thirst quencher, such an outcome would at least *seem* more probable…

I part cherry brandy
I part orange liqueur
Chilled lemonade
Ice

Stir the brandy and orange liqueur with ice into a highball or rocks glass. Add as much lemonade as you like.

MAE WEST

"Beulah, peel me a grape."
MAE WEST IN *I'M NO ANGEL* (1933)

Who can resist the wayward charm of this inimitable actress? Like its namesake, the Mae West cocktail must be treated with respect, so go easy on the cayenne pepper!

2 parts brandy
¹/₂ egg yolk
¹/₂ teaspoon sugar
Ice
Pinch of cayenne pepper,
  to finish

Shake with ice then strain into a frosted cocktail glass. Sprinkle with the cayenne pepper.

METROPOLITAN

2 parts brandy
2 parts vermouth
Dash of Angostura bitters
Dash of sugar syrup
Ice

Shake all the ingredients with ice and strain into a frosted cocktail glass.

HORSE'S NECK

The lemon spiral is the source of this cocktail's name, a comparison stemming from the way a bridle hangs from a horse. For my money, the cocktail should be called a Pig's Tail, but perhaps this wouldn't hold quite the same appeal…

2 parts brandy
4 parts ginger ale
Dash of Angostura bitters
Ice
1 lemon peel spiral

Pour the brandy over ice, then stir in the ginger ale and bitters before finishing off with your lemon spiral.

SIR WALTER COCKTAIL

(Sometimes known as the "Swalter," for obvious reasons.)

Walter Scott, author of *Waverley* and one of the founding fathers of the European novel, spent his early life on the rugged Scottish borders. It was there that he first developed a taste for brandy, which arrived in kegs smuggled over from the shores of the Solway.

1 part brandy
1 part rum
1 teaspoon grenadine
1 teaspoon curaçao
1 teaspoon lemon juice
Ice

Shake with ice and strain into a chilled cocktail glass.

AU REVOIR

"Adieu, adieu, to you and you and you!"

Au Revoir is the ideal end to a perfect day. Take it to bed with your favorite novel and enjoy a moment of decadence in the name of literature!

1 part brandy
1 part sloe gin
Juice of 1 lemon
1 egg white
Ice
Lemon or lime slice

Add the brandy, gin, lemon juice, and egg white, in that order, to ice in your shaker. Shake and strain into a cocktail glass. Garnish with the citrus slice of your choice.

VODKA-BASED COCKTAILS

"The house was overgrown with acacias. It stood near the fields, with limitless blue sky above it. Invisible cicadas were chirping in the grass as we sat outside, around a crude wooden table, and drank vodka."
FROM *BORDER'S UP! EASTERN EUROPE THROUGH THE BOTTOM OF A GLASS* BY VITALI VITALIEV

Vodka comes from Poland, where it was traditionally a medicinal drink, but soon became a social tonic, too. Viewed by many Poles as being integral to their way of life, vodka was even rationed there during the 1970s. Since the collapse of communism, consumption has risen 40 percent.

Elsewhere, vodka has flourished for rather different reasons. Not only is it the base spirit of so many easy summer cocktails, but it has also benefited from some of the most imaginative marketing campaigns of recent years, along with the launch of alco-pop blends such as Smirnoff Ice. My personal favorite is Zlota vodka, a clear drink beset with flecks of gold, so that it looks a little like a swirling snowstorm in a shot glass. An original Gdansk recipe, not only is Zlota vodka the prettiest drink you're ever likely to taste, it also benefits the digestive system!

Despite its history, vodka has a lightness of touch and the ability to re-vivify, and lends itself well to those with a creative spirit. In *Let Them Call it Jazz*, Jean Rhys' collection of short stories, she notes the benefits of "…tippling on vodka while writing letters…"

SEA BREEZE

"**Mama would often forgo a beer in favor of a vodka and grapefruit juice, which she kept in a squat aqua-and-white thermos. Across the front of the little thermos she had written with a freezer pen: RE-VIVIFICATION TONIC.**"

VIVI'S PICNIC DRINK IN *THE DIVINE SECRETS OF THE YA-YA SISTERHOOD* BY REBECCA WELLS

Top off Vivi's flask with some cranberry juice and, hey presto, you've got yourself a delicious Sea Breeze.

1 part vodka
2 parts cranberry juice
2 parts grapefruit juice
Ice

Pour the vodka over ice in a tall glass. Add the juices and stir.

BLACK RUSSIAN

Ninotchka (Greta Garbo):
"I must have a detailed
  report of your negotiations
  and a detailed expense
  account."
Buljanoff (Felix Bressart):
"No, non, Ninotchka. Don't
  ask for it. There is an old
  Turkish proverb that says,
  if something smells bad,
  why put your nose to it?"
**Ninotchka: "There is an old
  Russian saying, the cat
  who has cream on his
  whisker had better find
  good excuses."**

2 parts Russian vodka
1 part Kahlua
Maraschino cherry
Ice

Shake with ice and pour into
a rocks glass.

From *Ninotchka*, the 1939 comedy
screenplay by Billy Wilder, in which
the Black Russian is deployed as a
potent prop. Well, if it's good enough
for Greta…

WHITE RUSSIAN

2 parts Russian vodka
1 part Kahlua
1 part light cream
Ice

Shake with ice and pour into a
rocks glass.

Tip
For a less calorific take on this
cocktail, try using milk instead
of cream.

BLOODY MARY

Bloody Mary's are an acquired taste, and like stout beer, can sometimes be the perfect short-term alternative to a meal! Often drunk "the morning-after," there are numerous variations of this revitalizing drink, and it is one which you will find any bartender worth his salt willing to debate about!

2 parts ice-cold tomato juice
I part vodka
Dash of Worcestershire sauce
Pinch of black pepper
Lots of ice

Add all ingredients to a rocks glass and serve while cold.

Tip
Optional ingredients include pepper, celery salt, horseradish, celery stick, Tabasco sauce, lemon juice, and ketchup.

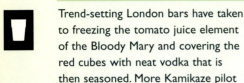

BLOODY NORA

Trend-setting London bars have taken to freezing the tomato juice element of the Bloody Mary and covering the red cubes with neat vodka that is then seasoned. More Kamikaze pilot than road to recovery…

2 parts vodka
4 or more tomato juice ice cubes
Dash of Worcestershire sauce
Pinch of black pepper

Take a rocks glass and pour the vodka over the tomato ice cubes (made by freezing tomato juice in an ice tray) and add the sauce and black pepper.

COSMOPOLITAN

3 parts vodka (lemon-flavor works well)
3 teaspoons Triple Sec
I part cranberry juice
Dash of fresh lime juice
Ice
Twist of orange peel

Shake all the ingredients with ice and pour into a chilled cocktail glass. Finish with a twist of orange peel.

HARVEY WALLBANGER

2 parts vodka
I part Galliano
Chilled orange juice
Ice
Slice of lemon

Pour the vodka and Galliano into an ice-filled tall glass. Top up with orange juice and garnish with lemon slice.

Tip
Replacing vodka with tequila makes a Freddy Fudpucker.

LONG ISLAND ICED TEA

I part vodka
I part gin
I part tequila
I part light rum
3 to 4 parts chilled cola
I part lime juice
$1/2$ part Cointreau
I teaspoon sugar syrup
Ice
Slice of lemon
Fresh mint

Pour all the ingredients into an ice-filled highball glass and stir. Add the lemon slice and fresh mint to garnish.

MOSCOW MULE

2 parts vodka
1 part lime juice
Ginger ale
Ice
Slice of lemon

Stir the vodka and lime juice over ice in a highball glass. Top up with the ginger ale and garnish with lemon slice.

GRASSHOPPER

1 part vodka
1 part crème de menthe
1 part crème de cacao
Ice

Shake with ice and strain into a chilled cocktail glass.

MARTINI COCKTAILS

That President Franklin D. Roosevelt's preferred cocktail after repealing Prohibition in 1933 was the Martini may be viewed as further evidence of the political potential of this elegant little drink!

The Martini is the most sophisticated cocktail, with a cast of distinguished devotees and an unspoken accompanying etiquette. An advertisement for Martinis in a post-Prohibition edition of *Vanity Fair* states that, "People are going back to civilized cocktails – Martinis." Even the aesthetic value of the Martini glass is regarded as conducive to the drink's purity. Which reminds me, one should always hold the glass by the stem, my dear!

And what of the drink itself? After Prohibition, only slight changes to the gin-to-vermouth ratio occurred. But through the 1940s and 1950s, bitters were phased out, vermouth was viewed as a trifle, and vodka became a viable alternative to gin, thanks to Smirnoff's persuasive advertising campaigns. With less vermouth, the martini became drier, with James Bond it became slicker, with the 1980s boom it was re-established as the urban gentleman's drink of choice. Now, the sacred cow is subject to the imagination of a new breed of mixologists, so that the dry Martini must sit side-by-side with a fresh melon Martini.

From David Niven's Vodka Martinis in *My Man Godfrey* (1957) to journalist duo Clark Gable and Constance Bennett's cocktails in *After Office Hours* (1935), the Martini has always scaled the heights of understated cool in Hollywood. And all this before James Bond, in *Dr No,* ordered,

"A medium Vodka dry Martini – with a slice of lemon peel. Shaken and not stirred."

DRY MARTINI

*"When I have a martini,
I feel bigger, wiser, taller.
When I have the second,
I feel superlative. When I
have more, there's no
holding me."*
WILLIAM FAULKNER

5 parts gin
1 part dry vermouth
Cracked ice
Olive

To ensure a suitably sublime Martini experience, always frost your glass first and fill your martini pitcher with cracked (not crushed) ice. Adding spirits should be an act of precision: pour your dry gin in first then wait for the "smoke" to settle before adding the vermouth. Stir brusquely then strain into your frosted cocktail glass.

John Doxat gives the following advice for the Martini drinker in *Shaken Not Stirred: the Dry Martini*:

"If you are an olive character, use high quality green ones, not the black variety – and of course never stuffed ones."

GIBSON

"When in funds, his favorite tipple was a big glass of gin with just a drop of vermouth."

So said John Booth of the infamous playwright Eugene O'Neill. Named after America's first glamor girl, Irene Gibson, whether or not O'Neill opted for the onions in this tart libation remains uncertain. O'Neill was renowned for his drunken escapades and frequented the bars that were to form the basis of *Harry Hope's Last Chance Saloon* and subsequently O'Neill's play, *The Iceman Cometh.*

2 1/2 parts gin
1 1/2 teaspoons dry vermouth
Ice
2 cocktail onions

Add the alcohol to a half-filled glass of ice, then stir and strain into a cocktail glass.

VODKA COCKTAIL

"One martini is alright, two is too many, three is not enough."
JAMES THURBER

2 parts vodka
1 part dry vermouth
Cracked ice

Prepare as you would a Dry Martini, simply replacing the gin base with vodka.

FRESH MELON MARTINI

"It's like skinny-dipping in a Nordic lake with Greta Garbo."

MARTINI CONNOISSEUR AND AUTHOR BARNABY CONRAD ON A GOOD MARTINI.

The Fresh Melon Martini, created by cocktail maestro Angus Winchester (Managing Director at International Playboy Bartenders), is a fragrant, cooling summer drink with a kick.

2 parts gin
Dash of gomme (see page 15)
Dash of Midori
1 cup diced watermelon
Ice

Pour the gomme and Midori into your shaker and add the melon. Muddle, by crushing with a rolling-pin until the watermelon is completely pulped. Add the gin and ice and shake hard. Then, strain into a chilled cocktail glass.

EMERSON

"The only reward of virtue is virtue."

RALPH WALDO EMERSON

1 1/2 parts dry gin
1 part sweet vermouth
Juice of 1/2 a lime
1 teaspoon maraschino liqueur
Ice

Pour the ingredients into a shaker half-filled with ice. Shake well and strain into a chilled cocktail glass.

TEQUILA-BASED COCKTAILS

"In the splendour of a
midday without obligations,
In the most towering
darkness of doubt
and confusion,
That is when tequila
cheers us with its lesson
of consolation,
It's infallible pleasure and
frank indulgence."

FROM *TEQUILA: PANEGYRIC AND
EMBLEM* BY ALVARO MUTIS,
TRANSLATED BY MARK SCHAFER.

It is said that optimistic Mexicans recommend tequila as, "a remedy for everything bad and to celebrate anything good."

Tequila, the base of that most rudimentary of cocktail rituals, the Slammer, smacks of masculinity, and a bygone bandit era unhindered by social mores. It has never been viewed as a particularly refined drink and has traditionally been favored by a younger generation of "work hard, play hard" cocktail drinkers in the West.

Even so, the Magical Realism genre of South American literature is infused with flights of fancy and fantasy which may be due, in part, to this potent spirit. Prior to being regulated, the drink was mildly hallucinogenic due to its mescal content. Ancient Aztec rituals strengthen the myth, since they used the sap of the wild blue maguey or mescal azul cactus to make a raw spirit known as pulque. The powerful effects of this drink gave it an elevated position within the spiritual and cultural traditions of the Aztec society.

The appeal of the worm at the bottom of the mescal bottle may lie in its association with danger and unfettered desires. To eat the worm resonates with a dozen literary legends, from the fall of Eve in the garden of Eden to the death of Cleopatra from the bite of an asp.

Like cognac or champagne, authentic tequila can only be made in one region of Mexico: Jalisco. Derived from the blue agave plant, Mexican law requires that tequila must contain 51 percent of the plant. There are now three major categories of tequila: Gold, Anejo, and White. Both Gold and Anejo tequila are usually aged in white oak casks and boast a better quality and flavor.

CAIPIRINHA

Pontiero: "Nice. Fine. A-h!
This rum of yours is great.
I could drink it by the
litre...Ah, munh-munh:
I'm joking. I'm only kojink,
munhamunhando. I feel
good."

Treece: "Good. Real nice.
Uh huh! This rum of
yours is real good.
I could drink it bye the
litre...Aaww, hum-and-haw:
just bletherin' on,
hummin'-and-hawin'.
Feeling just fine."

These translations of the same
excerpt from João Guimãraes Rosa's
novella *The Jaguar*, reveal how much
is left to the interpreter. But, Brazilian
writer Rosa did believe that "Life on
this planet is chaos."

Pragmatism must also be employed
when preparing a Caipirinha, since
this Brazilian drink is traditionally
made with a local spirit, cachaça, and
the local citrus fruit, limon (limes
with seeds).

1 part tequila
2 parts light rum
**1 lime, chopped into small
pieces**
**2 teaspoons gomme
(see page 15)**
Crushed ice

Place the lime pieces in a tumbler
and douse with gomme. Crush the
mixture so that the oil of the lime
blends with the sugar. Add the
crushed ice and spirits and stir.

MARGARITA

The Margarita has a history as deliciously cloudy and intoxicating as the drink itself. Was it the child of Dallas socialite Margarite Sames in 1948, or of showgirl Margorie King, whose allergy to alcohol was thwarted by an attentive bartender in Mexico who poured her tequila over shaved ice, lime juice, and Triple Sec?

3 parts golden tequila
1 part Triple Sec
3 parts lime juice
Ice
Wedge of lime
Coarse salt
Slice of lime

Frost the rim of a chilled cocktail glass by running a wedge of lime around the rim and twisting the upturned glass in a shallow dish of coarse salt. Shake up the rest of the ingredients in an ice-filled shaker and slowly strain into the prepared glass. Finish with a slice of lime.

BLUE MARGARITA

In 2001, Orlando's citizens were witness to the biggest Margarita in history, when a 7,000 gallon Margarita weighing over 32 tons became the world's largest cocktail.

2 parts tequila
I part lime juice
I part blue curaçao
I part Triple Sec
Ice
Wedge of lime
Coarse salt

Frost the rim of a chilled glass by running a wedge of lime around the rim and twisting the upturned glass in a shallow dish of coarse salt.

Pour all the ingredients into a cocktail shaker with lots of ice. Shake and strain into the prepared glass.

TEQUILA SUNRISE

2 parts tequila
4 parts orange juice
I part grenadine
Ice
Slice of orange
Maraschino cherry

Pour the orange juice and tequila into a cocktail shaker half-filled with ice. Shake well and strain over ice in a tall glass. Add the grenadine slowly, so that it sinks to the bottom of the glass. When it has settled, garnish with the orange slice and cherry and serve.

IMAGINATION

"There is no world I know that can compare with pure imagination."
WILLY WONKA IN *CHARLIE AND THE CHOCOLATE FACTORY* BY ROALD DAHL.

Perhaps the hallucinatory properties of mescal, from which tequila is made, were inspiration for this whimsical title. An Imagination is on a par with a Piña Colada as a creamy after-dinner drink.

1 part tequila
2 parts curaçao
2 parts coconut milk
2 parts heavy cream
Crushed Ice

Pour the ingredients into a cocktail shaker half-filled with crushed ice. Shake imaginatively then strain into a cocktail glass.

TEQUILA MOCKINGBIRD

"Shoot all the bluejays you want, if you can hit 'em, but remember it's a sin to kill a mockingbird."

FROM *TO KILL A MOCKINGBIRD* BY HARPER LEE.

2 parts tequila
¹/₂ part lemon juice
1 teaspoon crème de menthe
Ice

Pour the ingredients into an ice-filled cocktail shaker. Shake it like you mean to kill the contents (sorry!) then slowly strain into a cocktail glass.

TEQUILA SLAMMERS

"The tequila had gone down nicely, as it always did. He wondered how the hell he'd live without tequila. Other drinks were fine but the short shot of the colorless liquid was the ace."

FROM *TEQUILA MAN* BY JOHN BLAZE

Tequila
Salt
Lime wedges

Drinking tequila slammers may seem as basic as Blaze's prose, but people often forget the right order. So here's how to do it like Tequila Man. Lick a pinch of salt from your hand, down your tequila shot, and then suck on the lime wedge.

ABSINTHE-BASED COCKTAILS

*"To me, absinthe became ...
as intriguing and
unrepentantly cool as
smoking opium or eating
lotuses.*

*The lure of absinthe
    is decadence
Paris at midnight,
    strange poetry,
The virgin, empty glass
    implores you."*

FROM *THE FLAVOR OF ABSINTHE*
BY JASON DEBOER.

This luminous concoction has a longstanding association with literary life. Purveyors of the drink and its concomitant lifestyle include writers Baudelaire, Poe, Wilde, Huysmans, and Strinberg, and artists Van Gogh, Degas, Manet, Picasso, and Gaugin.

A deceptively seductive drink, absinthe has an allure that overshadows its dangerous potential. A siren amongst drinks, the presence of the Green Fairy in drink folklore persisted during a long absence when it was unobtainable and illegal. It is the nerve-poison thujon, made from the toxic wormwood plant, which rendered the drink both hallucinogenic and a serious health risk, and which led to it being banned. Now, though, manufacturers of the drink must adhere to strict guidelines as to its content.

Like so many other spirits, absinthe's first use was medicinal. Utilized as a fever preventative by French troops fighting in Algeria in the mid-nineteenth century, the drink returned home to France with the serviceman where it found favor with "the masses" and intellectuals alike. During the "great collective binge" in Paris from 1880-1914, many found themselves in thrall to this emerald elixir.

It is hardly surprising that with such a following, the drink appeared to pose a threat to the status quo in the nineteenth century, so much so that absinthe was banned, partially because of its association with this potentially revolutionary element. Arguably, a rebellion sparked by absinthe never posed a real threat since the intoxicating effects were more likely to dissipate into fantasy rather than into direct action.

SAZERAC

This luminous blend was the perfect prop for the film *Beloved Infidel* (1959), based on F. Scott Fitzgerald's final desperate years, where personal misfortune took the form of alcoholism, a mentally ill wife and of course the perils of infidelity…

2 parts bourbon (rye whiskey)
Small dash of absinthe
1 white sugar cube soaked in
Angostura bitters
Soda water
Ice
Twist of lemon peel

Fill a rocks glass with ice, and then add the dash of absinthe; swill the absinthe and ice around the glass then discard. Place the Angostura-soaked cube in the glass and add soda. When dissolved, add ice and bourbon. Finish with a twist of lemon.

Tip
Pernod can be used instead of Absinthe.

WILDE MULE

1 part absinthe
Juice of 1 lime
Ginger ale
Ice

Pour the absinthe over ice in a rocks or highball glass. Add the lime juice and top off with ginger ale.

DEEP SEA

I dash of absinthe
I dash of orange bitters
I part French vermouth
I part gin
Olive
Lemon peel

Shake well and strain into a cocktail glass. Add an olive and twist a lemon peel on top.

DEPTH CHARGE

"Absinthe has a wonderful color, green. A glass of absinthe is as poetical as anything in the world. What difference is there between a glass of absinthe and a sunset?"
OSCAR WILDE

2 dashes of absinthe
I part lillet
I part dry gin
Orange peel

Shake well and strain into a cocktail glass. Add a twist of orange peel.

EDEN'S APPLE

"But in the end she is as bitter as wormwood, and as sharp as a two-edged sword."
THE BIBLE, PROVERBS 5:4

That absinthe is derived from bitter wormwood implies the existence of some form of the drink in Biblical times. Don't worry, though; there is nothing bitter about an Eden's Apple, a tangy yet sweet drink created by Johan Svensson of the Kensington Roof Garden bar in London.

1 part absinthe
3 teaspoons Midori
3 teaspoons Green Chartreuse
Apple juice
Ginger ale
Ice
Apple slice

Shake the absinthe, Midori, and Green Chartreuse with ice. Pour into a glass, add a splash of apple juice, then top off with the ginger ale. Garnish with the apple slice.

ABSINTHE FRIENDS

This recipe comes courtesy of Sebor, absinthe manufacturers.

2 parts blueberry liqueur
1 part absinthe
Crushed ice

Pour over crushed ice.

BULL RUSH

1 part absinthe
1 part vodka
4 parts Red Bull
Ice

Pour the absinthe and vodka over ice in a tall glass, then top up with Red Bull.

HEMINGWAY'S DREAM

"One cup of it took the place of the evening papers of all the old evenings in cafes, of all chestnut trees that would be in bloom now in this month..."

FROM *FOR WHOM THE BELL TOLLS* BY ERNEST HEMINGWAY

It is only fitting that the master of such ceremonies, Papa Hemingway, should have his very own blend. Thanks to Tim Goodfellow at Momo's for this recipe.

1 part absinthe
3 teaspoons lemon juice
3 sugar cubes
8 mint leaves
Ice

Put the ingredients in a cocktail shaker with ice. Shake vigorously then strain into a cocktail glass.

CHAMPAGNE AND WINE COCKTAILS

"Drink thy flask of Champaign, 'twill serve you for paint and love potion." RESTORATION PLAYWRIGHT ETHEREGE'S PLEDGES FOR CHAMPAGNE IN *SHE WOULD IF SHE COULD.*

Wine cocktails have a deceptive lightness of touch which often misleads the drinker into thinking they should refill their glass *ad infinitum*. As Hemingway's view of *Death in the Afternoon* (see page 78) attests to, it is all too easy to start drinking a sublime wine blend and continue until…well, for rather too long.

During the prohibition era, Flute Champagne Bar in New York City was an infamous speakeasy frequented by flappers and *bon vivants*. Now, such events are relived on theme nights at this Manhattan joint, during which your Champagne cocktails will be unceremoniously served in a mug! So the appeal of the illicit continues….

Dry, or brut, Champagne works best for drinks in this section because of the sweet mixers and fruits that are used to produce the cocktails. If you can't use brut, try extra dry, which, oddly is not as dry as brut, but do try to avoid using sec or demi-sec, or sparkling wines, as these are much sweeter. You should also note that Champagne fizzes madly when you pour it into a glass – and if you have forgotten you will soon be reminded. To avoid losing the fizz early or spilling the precious drink, be patient and pour slowly.

There is some debate about the source of Champagne cocktails. Gary Regan and Mardee Haidin Regan of *Wine Enthusiast* magazine argue that the drink is probably American. That Champagne's origins in the Champagne region of France leads one to suppose that adulterations to the drink were wont to begin where the wine ran most freely…

CHAMPAGNE COCKTAIL

"We'll always have Paris."

Rick Blain (Humphrey Bogart) to Ilsa Lund (Ingrid Bergman) in the 1942 classic *Casablanca*. Blain and Lund shared a Champagne cocktail at La Belle Aurore in Paris.

I part brandy
Champagne
I sugar cube
2 to 3 dashes Angostura bitters

It is said that the original Champagne cocktail was simply a blend of a sugar cube soaked in Angostura bitters and then drenched in Champagne. But combine this with brandy, and you have a drink of unquestionably understated elegance.

Place the sugar cube in a Champagne flute and soak in Angostura. Add the brandy before topping up slowly with Champagne.

BELLINI

[To a lady] *"...Wine awakens and refreshes the lurking passions of the mind, as varnish does the colors that are sunk in a picture, and brings them all out in their natural glowings."*
ALEXANDER POPE

The Bellini is one of the most delectably pure cocktails in existence. With only excellent Champagne and fresh peaches making up this exquisite blend, surely this nectar of the gods must be good for you?

Harry's Bar in Venice, Italy is said to be the birthplace of the Bellini, and I have heard high praise from many devotees who tell me he will never tell the secret of his inimitable blend.

**1 bottle chilled Champagne
3 or 4 ripe peaches**

Blanch the peaches and peel the skin off. Remove the pits and blend the fruit with plenty of ice. Transfer to a glass or crystal punch bowl and slowly top off with the Champagne.

Tip
You might also like to try this recipe with nectarines, mangos, or papaya instead of peaches.

BLACK VELVET

"I consumed in our time more oysters and smoked salmon, Champagne, Black Velvet or Pouilly Fumée than I have swallowed in the rest of my life"
JOCELYN RICKARDS ON TIME SPENT WITH LOVER GRAHAM GREENE.

Half Champagne
Half Guinness

Pour the chilled Guinness and Champagne into a tall glass simultaneously. You may need a friend to assist, which shouldn't prove too difficult. The simple but smooth drink is best enjoyed in good company!

Tip
You can use Cava, or another sparkling white wine, instead of Champagne, and Murphys, or another type of stout, instead of Guinness.

BUCK'S FIZZ

"I'm only a beer teetotaller, not a Champagne teetotaller."
FROM *CANDIDA*, ACT 3, BY GEORGE BERNARD SHAW

The Buck's Fizz cocktail was invented in 1921 at the Buck's club in London. The drink starred alongside Fred and Ginger in the film *Top Hat* (1935).

2 parts chilled Champagne
1 part fresh orange juice
Twist of orange peel

Pour the orange juice into a chilled flute, then slowly top off with Champagne. Garnish with a twist of orange peel.

MIMOSA

"They made a pitcher of Mimosas and a platter of prosciutto and cantaloupe, and sat on the deck."
FROM *THE DIVINE SECRETS OF THE YA-YA SISTERHOOD* BY REBECCA WELLS.

So many of the memorable moments in this novel revolve around indulging in well-planned eating and drinking events. The Mimosa is the perfect drink for society lady Vivi, even more so because it was created in 1925 at the Ritz Hotel in Paris. In essence, it is a lighter take on the Buck's Fizz.

3 parts chilled Champagne
3 parts orange juice
Twist of orange peel

Pour the Champagne and orange juice into a chilled flute. Add a twist of orange peel.

Tip
Create a Grand Mimosa by adding half a part of Cointreau.

THE FLAPPER

Niall Cowan of the Claridge Hotel in Rome created this delightful blend. Bar manager Paolo Loureiro notes that, "It tastes and feels healthy" which is recommendation enough to indulge oneself.

Champagne
1/2 part crème de cassis
6 ripe strawberries, 5 of them hulled
2 ice cubes

Place the hulled strawberries, crème de cassis, and ice into a blender and puree. Pour into a Champagne flute and top off slowly with Champagne. Stir gently and garnish with the final strawberry.

THE FRIZZANTINO

"A cause may be inconvenient, but it's magnificent. It's like Champagne or high heels, and one must be prepared to suffer for it."

FROM *THE TITLE* BY ARNOLD BENNETT.

This cocktail is as frivolous as its name and its place of origin, the Bellagio Hotel in Las Vegas.

Chilled Italian sparkling wine
3/4 ounce Campari
Curaçao
I sugar cube

Soak the sugar cube in curaçao, then place at the bottom of a Champagne flute. Pour over the Campari then top off with the sparkling wine and serve.

CLARET CUP

"He had a vineyard where he made 'tafetta' wines, soft and velvety."
FRANCOIS RABELAIS DESCRIBING THE WINE OF THE CHINON REGION OF FRANCE.

4 to 6 servings

2 pints claret wine
2 parts maraschino liqueur
4 parts curaçao
2 tablespoons superfine sugar

Pour the ingredients into a bowl with lots of ice. Stir until the sugar has dissolved.

DEATH IN THE AFTERNOON

Ernest Hemingway's contribution to the 1935 drink book, *Breath in the Afternoon* was Death in the Afternoon, though his particular version was made with absinthe, not pastis.
He suggests three to five should be drunk in succession, to which the editor of the volume adds, "after six of these cocktails The Sun Also Rises".

I part pastis
Chilled Champagne

Pour the pastis into a Champagne flute and slowly top off with Champagne.

Tip
Try this Hemingway-style by replacing pastis with absinthe.

FRENCH 75

Legend has it that the French 75 was born during the First World War. Henry, of Henry's Bar in Paris, named the drink in honor of the French 75 light field gun.

5 parts Champagne
1 part gin
1 part lemon juice
1 sugar cube
Ice
$^1/_2$ a slice of lemon
1 maraschino cherry

Pour the gin and lemon juice into a tall glass. Add the sugar cube and stir until it dissolves, then fill the glass with ice and top off with Champagne. Garnish with the halved lemon slice and cherry and serve with two or three straws.

SUMMER CUPS
AND COOLERS

"After a boisterous afternoon in the swimming pool, followed by a glorious ride on horseback over the mountains or up or down the Valley of the Moon, I found myself so keyed and splendid that I desired to be more highly keyed, to feel more splendid. I knew the way. A cocktail before supper was not the way. Two or three, at the very least, was what was needed."

FROM *JOHN BARLEYCORN* BY JACK LONDON.

Cups and punches are capable of capping a sublime spot in time. Such cocktails recall sparkling memories and awaken the senses in the same way that the smell of freshly cut grass or a favorite tune does. Summer is the time to bask in such life-affirming pleasures. Drinking a Zombie in snowy Newfoundland was never quite the same as a Sea Breeze on Brighton beach or a Piña Colada in the Caribbean.

This section differs slightly from the others with regard to quantities. While most of the drinks prepared in this book are more than adequate for one person, and yet sufficient for two, punches are notably informal drinks for sharing, so I have included several recipes which cater to greater numbers. Blends such as Cider Cup (page 85) are perfect for an impromptu gathering with a few close friends, whereas Toledo Punch (page 83) amply caters to a larger party. Just remember not to be tempted to add ad hoc offerings from guests into your punch; if you make something chilled, fresh, and delicious, your soirée's success is guaranteed!

Proceed no further if you are unwilling to invest in the essentials – namely ripe, fresh fruit. And stock up on ice – it always runs out early.

PIMMS

"You can't kiss away a murder"

But you can sip away a summer. Pimms makes an appearance in the 1944 film *Double Indemnity*. An adaptation by Billy Wilder and Raymond Chandler of James Cain's short story, this literary film noir steers clear of clichés, such as the whiskey-drinking investigator, by opting for this summer cup instead.

A simple ruby-red cocktail base, not dissimilar from the Gin Sling, Pimms No. 1 Cup was first made in 1840 but continues to be popular today, particularly in tennis-playing circles.

2 parts Pimms
1 part gin
Lemonade
Slice of lemon
Slice of orange
Cucumber peel
Sprig of fresh mint

Pour the gin and Pimms into a highball glass. Top off with lemonade and add the lemon, orange, and cucumber, finishing off with a sprig of mint. This drink deserves a swizzle stick.

LIME GALORE

This is a boys' own blend, which David Williams, drinks expert and writer for Harpers' *Wine and Spirit Weekly*, insists is a perfect thirst quencher. Apparently it has taken Shanghai by storm…

8 parts lager beer
2 parts fresh lime juice
Ice
Pepper

Mix the lager and lime juice briefly in a mixing glass, then pour slowly over ice in a cocktail or margarita glass frosted with pepper.

WATERMELON VODKA

This is an impressive party showpiece and far superior to the flavored fruit vodkas now swamping the market. But you do need a few days to prepare it.

I ripe watermelon
I bottle good quality vodka
Funnel

Cut a hole in the top of the melon, through which the funnel is to be inserted. Make sure it's a tight fit, or the precious vodka will leak out! Pour some vodka in. The fruit's flesh is absorbent, so you can add more over the next couple of days, until it's saturated. When it's "ripe," slice it up and serve.

Tip
To check for ripeness, see if the ends of the melon "give" a little when pressed. You should also be able to *smell* the melon, which is an indication that it is ready.

BRAMBLE

This is one of cocktail maestro Dick Bradsell's scrumptious inventions.

2 parts gin
1/2 part gomme
1/2 part Crème de Mure
1 part fresh lemon juice
Blackberries

Fill a tumbler with ice, add the gin, juice, and gomme, then shake. Strain over crushed ice and add the Crème de Mure. Garnish with fresh blackberries.

TOLEDO PUNCH

Created by Harry Johnson in 1882, this punch will have you on the ropes in no time! Think big and plan carefully, as the ingredients below should suffice for several dozen friends. Add a block of ice and serve in wine glasses. Just right for a slow-burning barbeque on long summer days. This recipe will serve 8 to 12.

1 pint cognac or brandy
1 3/4 pints soda water
Juice of 2 lemons
1/2 lb sugar
2 oranges, thinly sliced
1/2 a pineapple, diced
8 strawberries, hulled and halved
1 handful of fresh mint leaves

Put all the ingredients into a large punch bowl and dissolve the sugar. Then, add the ingredients below, pouring in the sparkling wine slowly, and last.

5 pints water
1 pint brandy
2 bottles of red wine
2 bottles of white wine
3 bottles of Champagne or cava

MINT JULEP

"Epicures rub the lips of the tumbler with a piece of fresh pineapple, and the tumbler itself is very often incrusted outside with stalactites of ice. As the ice melts, you drink."

According to cocktail folklore, this American drink was taken to England by British novelist Captain Marryat in the nineteenth century. This is the English version of the cocktail which uses the British favorite – brandy – in place of the American favorite bourbon. If you can't get hold of stalactites, regular ice cubes will suffice!

1 part brandy
2 teaspoons water
1 teaspoon white sugar
4 sprigs of mint
Fresh pineapple
Shaved ice
Straws

Dissolve the sugar with water in a Collins or other tall glass. Fill with shaved ice and add the brandy. Stir until the glass is heavily frosted, adding more ice if necessary. Decorate with fresh mint and pineapple pieces.

Tips
Do not hold the mixing glass in your hand while mixing.
Other versions use whisky rather than brandy, so don't be afraid to experiment.
Use short straws so that drinkers buries their nose in the fresh mint.

CIDER CUP

"Never to be forgotten, that first long secret drink of golden fire, juice of those valleys and of that time, wine of wild orchards, of russet summer, of plump red apples."

FROM *CIDER WITH ROSIE*
BY LAURIE LEE

Lee learned early the pleasures of drinking and viewed it as "one of the natural privileges of living." His writing is replete with references to the social and spiritual elevations inspired by alcohol, from cider in Somerset to cognac and sherry in Spain in the 1930s, as evidenced by his captivating novel *As I Walked Out One Midsummer Morning*.

4 to 6 servings

1 part maraschino liqueur
1 part curaçao
1 part brandy
2 pints medium-dry hard cider
Ice

Pour all your ingredients over lots of ice in a large glass pitcher or bowl.

Tip
Try adding seasonal fruits to finish.

BLACK CURRANT VODKA

1 pint of black currants
3 cups vodka

Place the black currants in a pitcher and pour in the vodka. Allow to stand for at least 24 hours, then strain the vodka back into the bottle and place in the freezer. Serve in iced shot glasses or poured over sorbet.

You can do this with blackberries and other soft summer fruits.

CLEAN-CUT COCKTAILS

Vincent: "Did you just order a five-dollar shake?"

Mia: "Sure did."

Vincent: "A shake? Milk and ice cream?"

Mia: "Uh-huh."

Vincent: "It cost five dollars?"

Mia: "Yep."

Vincent: "You didn't put bourbon in it or anything?"

Mia: "Nope."

Vincent: "Just checking."

VINCENT (JOHN TRAVOLTA) AND MIA (UMA THURMAN) LIMBERING UP FOR THEIR TURN ON THE DANCE FLOOR IN QUENTIN TARANTINO'S *PULP FICTION* (1994).

Mia's five-dollar shake will come as no surprise to smoothie converts. After all, these delicious drinks power many of us who can't seem to find the time to eat all the fresh fruit and veggies that we should. They're also the best thing ever if, like me, the idea of fruit is appealing, but you just don't get around to eating it. For such would-be health nuts, the smoothie is a savior.

SIMPLE SMOOTHIE BASE

To create classic fruit cocktails, you need these base ingredients to which you can add your favorite fruits.

Serves 2

1 banana
Glass of ice
1/2 **pint light cream**

Tip
Replace the cream with yogurt for a healthier take. If it's not sweet enough, add a teaspoon of honey.

FINNEGAN'S WAKE-UP CALL!

"Phall if you but will, rise you must: and none so soon either shall the pahrce for the nunce come to a setdown secular phoenish."
FROM *FINNEGANS WAKE*
BY JAMES JOYCE

I love the rich color of this smoothie, which I've named after Joyce's incomprehensible novel. Drink it on its own for breakfast, or enjoy it as a pick-me-up before relaxing into a lazy Sunday.

1 quantity smoothie base
1 handful raspberries
2 handfuls strawberries

Drop the fruits into the base mix (see above) in your blender, blend, and pour into a tall glass.

PIÑA LIBRE

Everyone knows that the "drinkability" of a good Piña Colada comes from its thirst-quenching, scrumptious, sweet, and almost entirely unalcoholic flavor. So here's my adaptation of the original, minus the rum.

I part pineapple juice
I part coconut cream
Crushed ice
Pineapple chunk
Maraschino cherry

Pour the pineapple juice, followed by the coconut cream, into a shaker half-filled with crushed ice. Shake, then pour into a tall glass. Garnish with the pineapple chunk and cherry.

CRANBERRY COOLER

1/2 part cranberry juice
1/2 part orange juice
Sparkling mineral water
Ice
Twist of orange peel

Pour the juices over lots of ice in a tall glass then top off with mineral water. To finish, add that twist of orange peel.

REAL LEMONADE

"I get no kick from champagne,
Mere alcohol doesn't thrill me at all,
So tell me why should it be true
That I get a kick out of you?"
FROM THE SONG "I GET A KICK OUT OF YOU' BY COLE PORTER (1934).

Real lemonade is to die for and bears no resemblance or comparison to the store bought variety.

3 to 4 tablespoons sugar
1/2 cup water (for boiling)
1 1/2 tablespoons fresh lemon juice
Pinch of salt
2 pints water
Ice
Fresh mint leaves
Lemon slices

Pour the sugar and water in a pan and boil for two minutes. Chill, then stir in the lemon juice and salt. Transfer to a large pitcher and add approximately 2 pints water. Add the mint and lemon slices and serve with lots of ice.

TWIST IN THE TAIL

The golden rule for budding writers is to master the twist in the tail.

2 large bananas
2 limes, juice and grated zest of both
Ginger ale
Sugar
Ice

Cut the banana into chunks and place in a blender. Add the lime juice, zest, sugar, and a little ginger ale. Pour over crushed ice in a tall glass then top off with ginger ale to taste.

LATE-NIGHT SPECIALS

"Great spirits have always
encountered violent
opposition from mediocre
minds."
ALBERT EINSTEIN

I realize this Einstein was probably
not referring to his favorite tipple
here but, whatever; it's late, you're
tired, conversations are drifting, and
all statements have at least two
meanings. Either go to bed or try
one of these …

EGG NOG

R. S. Surtee, Charles Dickens's
contemporary, was partial to a drop
of brandy and a toast or two:
"They drank to each other's
health, then the health of
the hounds."

Drunk warm, I can imagine no better
reviver than Egg Nog on a chilly
winter's day.

2 parts brandy
2 parts milk
I egg
I tablespoon of superfine sugar
Ice
Freshly grated nutmeg

Shake the brandy, milk, egg, and sugar
with the ice. Strain into a highball and
sprinkle with nutmeg.

AARON

This is the Hebrew word for high mountains, but also translates as "with love."

For 2 to share

2 parts vodka
I part crème de cassis
I part Baileys
I part heavy cream
Dash of grenadine
Ice
Fresh cherries

Pour the vodka, crème de cassis, Baileys, and heavy cream, in that order into a shaker half-filled with ice. Shake and strain into a glass. You may add the grenadine to the mix in the shaker for a pink tinge, or into your glass for a cherry swirl through the heart of the cocktail. Garnish with cherries.

IRISH COCKTAIL OR NORA'S NIGHTCAP

"It was you yourself, you naughty shameless girl who first led the way."
FROM JAMES JOYCE'S LETTER TO HIS GREAT LOVE, NORA BARNACLE, IN 1909.

Nora's Nightcap is a veritable jewel from the emerald isle.

2 parts Irish whiskey
6 dashes of crème de menthe
3 dashes of Green Chartreuse
Maraschino Cherry

Shake the ingredients and strain into a chilled cocktail glass. Decorate with a cherry, if desired.

AFTER-SUPPER COCKTAIL

"That day we got no further with our reading."
FROM DANTE'S *INFERNO*, V:136

1 part apricot brandy
1 part Triple Sec
¹/₂ teaspoon lemon juice
Ice

Pour the ingredients over ice then shake well. Strain into a cocktail glass.

GOLDEN SLIPPER

Cinderella's cocktail is for drinking companions who threaten to leave before midnight.

1 part Green Chartreuse
2 parts apricot brandy
Ice

Stir with ice and strain into a cocktail glass.

Tip
Slip an unbroken egg yolk on top if you are brave enough. However, remember that eating raw egg carries a risk of salmonella (see page 2).

GLOSSARY

Cointreau
 – orange liqueur
Cordial médoc
 – distilled claret
Crème de cacao
 – cocoa liqueur
Crème de menthe
 – peppermint liqueur
Crème de Mure
 – blackberry liqueur
Curaçao
 – wine-based liqueur with orange
   peel
Danziger Goldwasser
 – sweet liqueur containing gold leaf
   which tastes of aniseed and
   orange. The silver version is much
   the same.
Drambuie
 - syrupy blend of Scotch and honey
Dubonnet
 – apéritif with a quinine taste
Green Chartreuse
 – an aromatic liqueur with a higher
   alcohol content than standard,
   yellow Chartreuse
Grenadine
 – sweet syrup made of
   pomegranate juice
Kirschwasser
 – liqueur distilled with kernels of
   cherry stones

Lillet
 – fortified white wine with
   Armagnac
Maraschino
 – made from Italian marasca
   cherries and flavored with the
   kernels, having a taste like bitter
   almonds
Midori
 – a Japanese liqueur, flavored
   with melon
Peychaud bitters
 – bitters from America
   (similar to Angostura)
Schnapps
 – sweet gin-style drink
Vermouth (sweet)
 – white wine infused with
   aromatic herbs
Vermouth (dry)
 – white wine infused with
   chamomile flowers

BIBLIOGRAPHY

Booth, John. *Creative Spirits: A Toast to Literary Drinkers* London: André Deutsch, 1997.

Cradock, Harry. *The Savoy Cocktail Book.* London: Mayflower Press, 1971.

Harwood, Jeremy. *Collins Gem Cocktails.* London: Collins, 1999.

Heaton, Vernon. *Cocktail Party Secrets.* Surrey: Elliot Right Way Books, 1963.

Goodall, Jonathan. *The Classic Bar & Cocktail Book.* London: Apple Press, 2001.

Mr. Boston Deluxe Bartender's Guide. Boston: Mr. Boston Distiller Corporation, 1978.

ABOUT THE AUTHOR

Anna Kiernan was born into a family with a stake in drink, since both her grandfather and father worked for Guinness in Dublin. Her interest in the union of writing and drinking resulted in "Cocktales," a literary cabaret night in a cocktail bar in London. She has edited and contributed to a number of books on drink, and her work has also appeared in *The Times Literary Supplement, Private Eye,* and *The Big Issue.*

ACKNOWLEDGMENTS

The publisher would like to thank the Riki-Tik Bar of Bond Street, Brighton, and especially Marcel Jackson, for being our expert mixologist. Credit goes to Becky Dewing who discovered Riki-Tik Bar after hours of research.

The images on pages 7 and 8 were kindly provided by The Algonquin Hotel and thanks go to Barbara McGurn for her interest and help.

INDEX